First edition for the United States and Canada published in 2003 by Barron's Educational Series, Inc.

First edition for Great Britain published 2003 by Hodder Wayland, a division of Hachette Children's Group, an Hachette UK Company

All inquiries should be addressed to:
Peterson's Publishing, LLC
8740 Lucent Blvd, Ste 400
Highlands Ranch, CO 80129
www.petersonsbooks.com

Library of Congress Catalog Card No. 2002111582

ISBN-13: 978-0-7641-2459-4
ISBN-10: 0-7641-2459-5
Date of Manufacture : April 2020
Manufactured by : Shenzhen Wing King Tong Paper Products Co. Ltd., Shenzhen, Guangdong, China

Printed in China
20 19 18 17 16

Disclaimer
The web site addresses (URLs) included in this book were valid at the time of going to press. However, because of the nature of the Internet, it is possible that some addresses may have changed, or sites may have changed or closed down since publication. While the publisher regrets any inconvenience this may cause readers, no responsibility for any such changes will be accepted by the publisher.

The Skin I'm In

A FIRST LOOK AT RACISM

PAT THOMAS
ILLUSTRATED BY LESLEY HARKER

B.E.S.

PUBLISHING

Imagine a world where only people with blue eyes could go to school. Or a world where only people with brown eyes could get a job.

If we lived
in a world like
this many people
would be treated
unfairly. They would
miss out on the chance to
learn and work and feel good
about themselves.

The way you look is decided by your family background.

Sometimes this is called your culture, or race. The most common way race is judged is by the color of your skin.

Your race tells the history of your family. It is where your ancestors come from and the religion and traditions your family has followed for many years.

What about you?

What do you know about your family's history?
What are the variety of skin colors
that people come in?

Our world is like a big, beautiful garden, filled with animals and plants of every color, shape and size.

People come in lots of beautiful colors, shapes, and sizes, too. And even though there are different races, we also belong to one big human family. We are all much more alike than different.

Some believe that people from their
race are worth more and should
be treated better than people from
other races. A person who thinks and acts
this way is called a racist.

Racists want to stop people of other races from living, working, and learning together.

Anybody of any skin color can be a racist .

Racists make it hard for us all to live together peacefully.

They are bullies who use the differences between people
as an excuse for calling names, picking fights, and
keeping other people from having equal human rights.

Like all bullies, racists are cowards. They are afraid of anybody who looks different from them.

Have you ever been afraid of somebody that looked different from you? It happens to everyone. But most people make the effort to get to know someone before they decide about them.

Racists never do this.

They always judge others
by how they look,
and not by who
they are.

Sometimes racist behavior is obvious. But sometimes it can be hidden in the way people treat each other or talk about each other.

You should never copy racist
behavior and, whenever you feel
you can, it is good to let others
know you think it is wrong.

When you are bullied by a racist for the color of your skin, you may feel as if you have done something wrong and wish you could be someone different.

It can make you feel sad and lonely and frightened. You may not want to eat or sleep, or leave the house or go to school.

What about you?

Have you ever been bullied because of your skin color?
Have you ever seen anyone bullied because of this?
How did it make you feel?

You may feel that no one will understand or believe you if you tell them what is happening.

But you must never keep racist behavior a secret.

Always tell an adult you
trust about it.

The people who love you
and care about you will
be able to help.

Racists only see the differences between people.

But most people know that it is okay for each of us
to look and act differently, and have different beliefs.

Most people want the
world to be a place where
each of us gets the same
opportunities to make friends
and to learn and grow.

25

But even though we may be of different races, science has shown that we share the same basic human makeup and so are mostly all alike.

Remember, the best way to make the world a fair and safe place for everyone to live is for people to appreciate the racial differences between them and how much everyone has in common.

HOW TO USE THIS BOOK

Racism is a complex issue that brings up a wide range of emotions in all of us. Children may be less able to express these emotions than adults. Parents and teachers con help in many ways. Here ore some simple guidelines:

Children who ore raised in a nurturing environment where they feel loved, supported, and valued hove the best chance of developing a good self-image. Those who feel good about themselves and confident of their place in the world ore less likely to be fearful or mistrustful of those who ore different from them. Likewise, if you ore respectful of all people, your children will follow your example.

Children who ore suffering racist abuse con find it as difficult to talk about as those who ore suffering any other kind of abuse. This is because racist attacks con make the victim feel ashamed of who they ore and lose their faith that anyone con help. A child who feels like this will need a great deal of support while they struggle to find the words to express what they ore feeling.

It is common for children who suffer racist abuse to feel ashamed of their race. Young children naturally seek assimilation rather than independence. This con be frustrating for parents who wish to instill a sense of racial pride in their children. Don't force the point, instead continue to lead by example. As your child grows older the need to be like others will be replaced by pride in his or her own individuality.

Racism is a form of prejudice. Talk with your children about prejudice in its wider context. This includes religious and sexual prejudice, prejudice against those with disabilities, and even the belief that adults are entitled to more human rights than children. Also while the common perception is that racism is directed at people of color by white people, this is not always true. As world events have shown, racism can also exist between people of the same color skin living in the same country.

There are many ways to teach appreciation of diversity. Try to answer all your child's questions about racial differences openly. Encourage open discussions about the ways in which we are all different and the ways in which we are all the same. In our multicultural society, we mix and match many aspects of other cultures, for example in what we eat, how we dress, and the music we listen to. Point these out to your children as examples of "common ground" with other cultures.

Schools are ideal places to help teach diversity and tolerance. Most of the time this is done indirectly, for instance by celebrating the holidays and festivals of many cultures and teaching about the traditions and foods of different cultures. Whenever possible teachers may wish to be more direct. Set up a "circle time" or similar discussion groups within the class where students can talk in general about important topics such as racism.

GLOSSARY

ancestors The members of your family that were born many years before you were.

judge To form an opinion, or have your own views about somebody or something.

race Any of the major groups into which human beings can be divided. People of the same race originally came from the same part of the world and often share characteristics, such as skin color, language, or religion.

racism The belief that one's race or culture is better than another and so entitled to more rights and opportunities.

traditions Customs, celebrations or ways of doing things that are passed on year after year, through the generations.

FURTHER READING

All the Colors of the Earth by Sheila Hamanaka (Morrow Junior Books, 1994)

America Street: A Multicultural Anthology of Stories by Anne Mazer (Perea Books, 1993)

Boys and Girls of the World: from one end...to the other by Núria Roca (Barron's Educational Series, Inc., 2002)

Hate Hurts by Caryl Stern-LaRosa and Ellen Hofheimer Bettmann (Scholastic Books, 2000)

Same Difference: Young Writers on Race edited by San Francisco Writerscorp (WritersCorps Books, 1998)

Under Our Skin: Kids Talk About Race by Debbie H. Birdseye (Holiday House, 1997)

Who Belongs Here? by Margy) Burns Knight (Tilbury House Publishers, 1993)

CONTACTS

American Civil Liberties Union
An organization devoted to defending and preserving the individual rights and liberties guaranteed to all people in this country by the Constitution and laws of the United States.
http://www.aclu.org

Anti-Defamation League of B'nai B'rith
823 United Nations Plaza, New York, New York 10017
http://www.adl.org

National Association for the Advancement of Colored People
http://www.naacp.org

ERIC—Curriculum to Reduce Racial Conflict
Website devoted to the use of curriculum to develop a climate for racial equality through multicultural education, anti-racist education, and conflict resolution.
http://www.eric-web.tc.columbia.edu